Millionaire Truck Driver

Starting at Age 22 - Married at 22

by

Hawkeye John

Milionaire Truck Driver: Starting at Age 22 - Married at 22

by Hawkeye John

Published in the USA

First publication date December, 2013

Available at Amazon.com
(Paperback and Kindle versions)

More Stuff

Twitter: @byHawkeyeJohn (follow me & I'll follow you)

Facebook: facebook.com/hawkeye.john.writer (friend me)

Website & blog: hawkeyejohn.com (bookmark for What's New)

Pinterest: pinterest.com/HawkeyeJohn (I'll follow your boards)

Dedicated to all the hard working Truck Drivers out there.

Table of Contents

Chapter 1

The Story of Joe

Joe begins his trucking career at the age of 22. He loves to drive trucks. Joe feels that he is providing a valuable service to people. Joe gets ecstatic about getting back on the road after a few days off. He gets married at 22. His wife works as a bookkeeper.

Joe and his wife buy a $200,000 house with cash when Joe turns 34. When Joe is age 35, they buy a car for $25,000 cash.

Joe's wife retires from her bookkeeping career when Joe is 36 years old. She becomes a full-time Mom. Joe retires at the age of 62. He and his wife accumulate $1,309,876 in cash and assets. They buy a $400,000 condo on the beach with cash. Joe and his wife also buy an RV camper for 100,000 cash. Joe still likes to drive long distances and the RV camper fills this void.

At 62 years old Joe and his wife have a monthly income of $4,000 tax-free. They continue to receive this $4,000 per month for the rest of their lives. They set up a trust. The trust will give $4,000 per month after they die to their favorite charity. The trust will keep giving this amount long after they are gone.

The rest of this book gives you a blueprint of how Joe and his wife accomplish their financial independence. The land of critical mass. Freedom!

Chapter 2

The 5 Rules to Follow

1. Give 10% of your income to your favorite charity. Why? Because it gives you the sense of abundance. It's a nice thing to do. It's giving back. In general, the more you give, the more you receive. It's giving thanks to the Higher Power. If you're a believer, it's giving thanks to God.
2. Contribute $250 every month to a Roth IRA (Individual Retirement Account). Invest this money in the Vanguard Total Stock Market Index Mutual Fund at https://investor.vanguard.com/home/. This investment has very low costs and has returned over 9% interest per year since its inception in 1992. In Joe's case, his investments returned an average of 9% interest per year. If the stock market is down, keep investing monthly. If the stock market is up, keep investing monthly.
3. Never borrow money. Pay cash for everything. Rent until you can buy it with cash.

4. Live below your means. Spend less than you make. Don't waste your hard earned money. Be frugal. Be creative. Sacrifice some luxuries now and hopefully you can enjoy them in abundance later without digging yourself into a hole.
5. Save money in your Piggy Bank for an emergency fund or an investment, such as a house.

Chapter 3

Millionaire Truck Driver: Starting Out at the Age of 22, Married at 22

Combined income per year = $48,000

Combined income per month = $4,000

- Give 10% of income to charity = $400 per month
- Contribute $250 per month to Roth IRA
- Put $850 per month in Piggy Bank

Money left over per month for expenses and taxes = $2,500

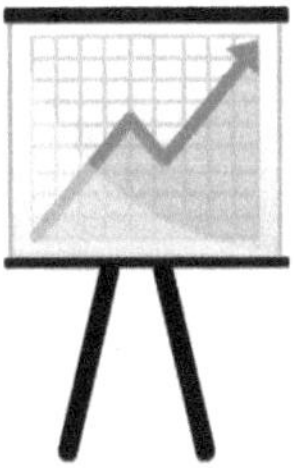

Portfolio at Age 22

- Roth IRA = $3,000
- Piggy Bank = $10,200

Total Portfolio Value = $13,200

Chapter 4

Age 23

Combined income per year = $50,000

Combined income per month = $4,167

- Give 10% of income to charity = $417 per month
- Contribute $250 per month to Roth IRA
- Put $950 per month in Piggy Bank

Money left over per month for expenses and taxes = $2,550

Portfolio at Age 23

- Roth IRA = $6,270
- Piggy Bank = $21,600

Total Portfolio Value = $27,870

Chapter 5

Age 24

Combined income per year = $52,000

Combined income per month = $4,333

- Give 10% of income to charity = $433 per month
- Contribute $250 per month to Roth IRA
- Put $1,050 per month in Piggy Bank

Money left over per month for expenses and taxes = $2,600

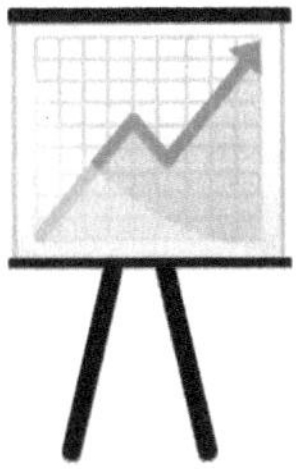

Portfolio at Age 24

- Roth IRA = $9,834
- Piggy Bank = $34,200

Total Portfolio Value = $44,034

Chapter 6

Age 25

Combined income per year = $54,000

Combined income per month = $4,500

- Give 10% of income to charity = $450 per month
- Contribute $250 per month to Roth IRA
- Put $1,150 per month in Piggy Bank

Money left over per month for expenses and taxes = $2,650

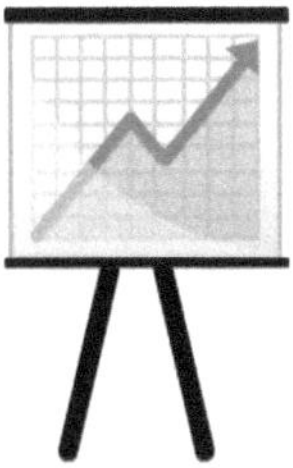

Portfolio at Age 25

- Roth IRA = $13,719
- Piggy Bank = $48,000

Total Portfolio Value = $61,719

Chapter 7

Age 26

Income per year = $56,000

Income per month = $4,667

- Give 10% of income to charity = $467 per month
- Contribute $250 per month to Roth IRA
- Put $1,250 per month in Piggy Bank

Money left over per month for expenses and taxes = $2,700

Portfolio at Age 26

- Roth IRA = $17,954
- Piggy Bank = $63,000

Total Portfolio Value = $80,954

Chapter 8

Age 27

Combined income per year = $58,000

Combined income per month = $4,833

- Give 10% of income to charity = $483 per month
- Contribute $250 per month to Roth IRA
- Put $1,350 per month in Piggy Bank

Money left over per month for expenses and taxes = $2,750

Portfolio at Age 27

- Roth IRA = $22,570
- Piggy Bank = $79,200

Total Portfolio Value = $101,770

Chapter 9

Age 28

Combined income per year = $60,000

Income per month = $5,000

- Give 10% of income to charity = $500 per month
- Contribute $250 per month to Roth IRA
- Put $1,450 per month in Piggy Bank

Money left over per month for expenses and taxes = $2,800

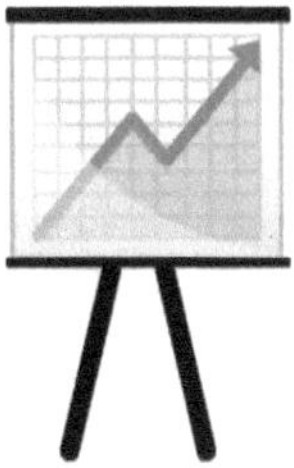

Portfolio at Age 28

- Roth IRA = $27,601
- Piggy Bank = $96,600

Total Portfolio Value = $124,201

Chapter 10

Age 29

Combined income per year = $62,000

Combined income per month = $5,167

- Give 10% of income to charity = $517 per month
- Contribute $250 per month to Roth IRA
- Put $1,550 per month in Piggy Bank

Money left over per month for expenses and taxes = $2,850

Portfolio at Age 29

- Roth IRA = $33,085
- Piggy Bank = $115,200

Total Portfolio Value = $148,285

Chapter 11

Age 30

Combined income per year = $64,000

Combined income per month = $5,333

- Give 10% of income to charity = $533 per month
- Contribute $250 per month to Roth IRA
- Put $2,050 per month in Piggy Bank

Money left over per month for expenses and taxes = $2,900

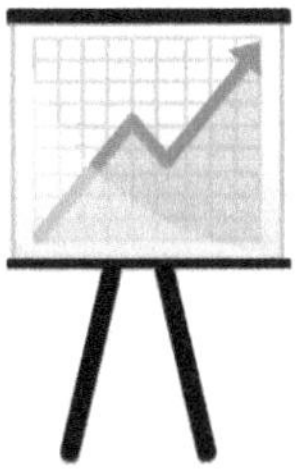

Portfolio at Age 30

- Roth IRA = $39,063
- Piggy Bank = $135,000

Total Portfolio Value = $174,063

Chapter 12

Age 31

Combined income per year = $66,000

Combined income per month = $5,500

- Give 10% of income to charity = $550 per month
- Contribute $250 per month to Roth IRA
- Put $1,750 per month in Piggy Bank

Money left over per month for expenses and taxes = $2,950

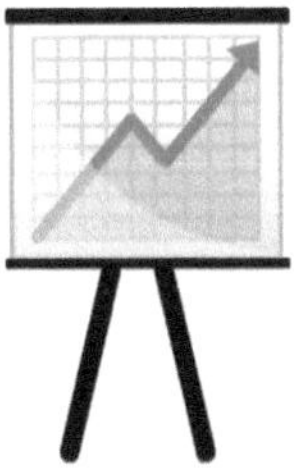

Portfolio at Age 31

- Roth IRA = $45,579
- Piggy Bank = $156,000

Total Portfolio Value = $201,579

Chapter 13

Age 32

Combined income per year = $68,000

Combined income per month = $5,667

- Give 10% of income to charity = $567 per month
- Contribute $250 per month to Roth IRA
- Put $1,850 per month in Piggy Bank

Money left over per month for expenses and taxes = $3,000

Portfolio at Age 32

- Roth IRA = $52,681
- Piggy Bank = $178,200

Total Portfolio Value = $230,881

Chapter 14

Age 33

Combined income per year = $70,000

Combined income per month = $5,833

- Give 10% of income to charity = $583 per month
- Contribute $250 per month to Roth IRA
- Put $1,950 per month in Piggy Bank

Money left over per month for expenses and taxes = $3,050

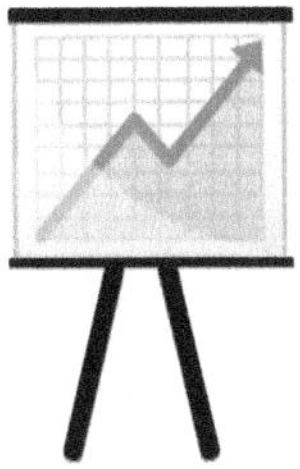

Portfolio at Age 33

- Roth IRA = $60,422
- Piggy Bank = $201,600

Total Portfolio Value = $262,022

Chapter 15

Age 34

Combined income per year = $72,000

Combined income per month = $6,000

- Give 10% of income to charity = $600 per month
- Contribute $250 per month to Roth IRA
- Put $2,050 per month in Piggy Bank
- Buy a house with cash from the Piggy Bank = $200,000

Money left over per month for expenses and taxes = $3,100

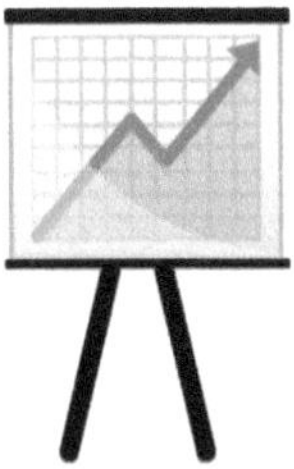

Portfolio at Age 34

- Roth IRA = $68,860
- Piggy Bank = $26,200
- House = $200,000

Total Portfolio Value = $295,060

Chapter 16

Age 35

Income per year = $74,000

Income per month = $6,167

- Give 10% of income to charity = $617 per month
- Contribute $250 per month to Roth IRA
- Put $2,150 per month in Piggy Bank
- Buy a car with cash from the Piggy Bank = $25,000

Money left over per month for expenses and taxes = $3,150

Portfolio at Age 35

- Roth IRA = $78,860
- Piggy Bank = $27,000
- House = $200,500
- Car = $25,000

Total Portfolio Value = $330,558

Chapter 17

Age 36

Income per year = $38,000

Income per month = $3,167

- Give 10% of income to charity = $317 per month
- Contribute $250 per month to Roth IRA
- Joe's wife retires and becomes a full-time mother

Money left over per month for expenses and taxes = $2,600

Portfolio at Age 36

- Roth IRA = $88,083
- Piggy Bank = $27,000
- House = $201,000
- Car = $24,000

Total Portfolio Value = $340,083

Chapter 18

Age 37

Income per year = $39,000

Income per month = $3,250

- Give 10% of income to charity = $325 per month
- Contribute $250 per month to Roth IRA

Money left over per month for expenses and taxes = $2,675

Portfolio at Age 37

- Roth IRA = $99,010
- Piggy Bank = $27,000
- House = $201,500
- Car = $23,000

Total Portfolio Value = $350,510

Chapter 19

Age 38

Income per year = $40,000

Income per month = $3,333

- Give 10% of income to charity = $333 per month
- Contribute $250 per month to Roth IRA

Money left over per month for expenses and taxes = $2,700

Portfolio at Age 38

- Roth IRA = $110,921
- Piggy Bank = $27,600
- House = $202,000
- Car = $22,000

Total Portfolio Value = $362,521

Chapter 20

Age 39

Income per year = $41,000

Income per month = $3,417

- Give 10% of income to charity = $342 per month
- Contribute $250 per month to Roth IRA
- Put $50 per month in Piggy Bank

Money left over per month for expenses and taxes = $2,775

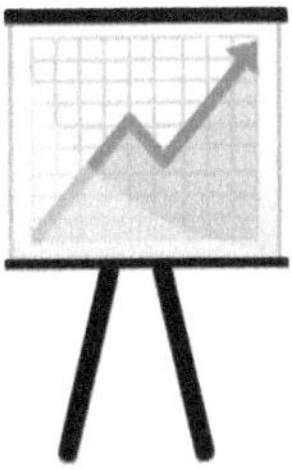

Portfolio at Age 39

- Roth IRA = $123,904
- Piggy Bank = $28,200
- House = $202,500
- Car = $21,000

Total Portfolio Value = $375,604

Chapter 21

Age 40

Income per year = $42,000

Income per month = $3,500

- Give 10% of income to charity = $350 per month
- Contribute $250 per month to Roth IRA
- Put $50 per month in Piggy Bank

Money left over per month for expenses and taxes = $2,850

Portfolio at Age 40

- Roth IRA = $138,055
- Piggy Bank = $28,800
- House = $203,000
- Car = $20,000

Total Portfolio Value = $389,855

Chapter 22

Age 41

Income per year = $43,000

Income per month = $3,583

- Give 10% of income to charity = $358 per month
- Contribute $250 per month to Roth IRA
- Put $50 per month in Piggy Bank

Money left over per month for expenses and taxes = $2,925

Portfolio at Age 41

Roth IRA = $153,480
Piggy Bank = $29,400
House = $203,500
Car = $19,000

Total Portfolio Value = $405,380

Chapter 23

Age 42

Income per year = $44,000

Income per month = $3,667

- Give 10% of income to charity = $367 per month
- Contribute $250 per month to Roth IRA
- Put $50 per month in Piggy Bank

Money left over per month for expenses and taxes = $3,000

Portfolio at Age 42

- Roth IRA = $170,294
- Piggy Bank = $30,000
- House = $204,000
- Car = $18,000

Total Portfolio Value = $422,294

Chapter 24

Age 43

Income per year = $45,000

Income per month = $3,750

- Give 10% of income to charity = $375 per month
- Contribute $250 per month to Roth IRA
- Put $50 per month in Piggy Bank

Money left over per month for expenses and taxes = $3,075

Portfolio at Age 43

- Roth IRA = $188,620
- Piggy Bank = $30,600
- House = $204,500
- Car = $17,000

Total Portfolio Value = $440,720

Chapter 25

Age 44

Income per year = $45,000

Income per month = $3,750

- Give 10% of income to charity = $375 per month
- Contribute $250 per month to Roth IRA
- Put $50 per month in Piggy Bank

Money left over per month for expenses and taxes = $3,075

Portfolio at Age 44

- Roth IRA = $208,596
- Piggy Bank = $31,200
- House = $205,000
- Car = $16,000

Total Portfolio Value = $460,796

Chapter 26

Age 45

Income per year = $45,000

Income per month = $3,750

- Give 10% of income to charity = $375 per month
- Contribute $250 per month to Roth IRA
- Put $50 per month in Piggy Bank

Money left over per month for expenses and taxes = $3,075

Portfolio at Age 45

- Roth IRA = $230,369
- Piggy Bank = $31,800
- House = $205,500
- Car = $15,000

Total Portfolio Value = $482,669

Chapter 27

Age 46

Income per year = $45,000

Income per month = $3,750

- Give 10% of income to charity = $375 per month
- Contribute $250 per month to Roth IRA
- Put $50 per month in Piggy Bank

Money left over per month for expenses and taxes = $3,075

Portfolio at Age 46

- Roth IRA = $254,103
- Piggy Bank = $32,400
- House = $206,000
- Car = $14,000

Total Portfolio Value = $506,502

Chapter 28

Age 47

Income per year = $45,000

Income per month = $3,750

- Give 10% of income to charity = $375 per month
- Contribute $250 per month to Roth IRA
- Put $50 per month in Piggy Bank

Money left over per month for expenses and taxes = $3,075

Portfolio at Age 47

- Roth IRA = $279,972
- Piggy Bank = $33,000
- House = $206,500
- Car = $13,000

Total Portfolio Value = $532,472

Chapter 29

Age 48

Income per year = $45,000

Income per month = $3,750

- Give 10% of income to charity = $375 per month
- Contribute $250 per month to Roth IRA
- Put $50 per month in Piggy Bank

Money left over per month for expenses and taxes = $3,075

Portfolio at Age 48

- Roth IRA = $308,169
- Piggy Bank = $33,600
- House = $207,000
- Car = $12,000

Total Portfolio Value = $560,769

Chapter 30

Age 49

Income per year = $45,000

Income per month = $3,750

- Give 10% of income to charity = $375 per month
- Contribute $250 per month to Roth IRA
- Put $50 per month in Piggy Bank

Money left over per month for expenses and taxes = $3,075

Portfolio at Age 49

- Roth IRA = $338,905
- Piggy Bank = $34,200
- House = $207,500
- Car = $11,000

Total Portfolio Value = $591,605

Chapter 31

Age 50

Income per year = $45,000

Income per month = $3,750

- Give 10% of income to charity = $375 per month
- Contribute $250 per month to Roth IRA
- Put $50 per month in Piggy Bank

Money left over per month for expenses and taxes = $3,075

Portfolio at Age 50

- Roth IRA = $372,406
- Piggy Bank = $34,800
- House = $208,000
- Car = $10,000

Total Portfolio Value = $625,206

Chapter 32

Age 51

Income per year = $45,000

Income per month = $3,750

- Give 10% of income to charity = $375 per month
- Contribute $250 per month to Roth IRA
- Put $50 per month in Piggy Bank

Money left over per month for expenses and taxes = $2,075

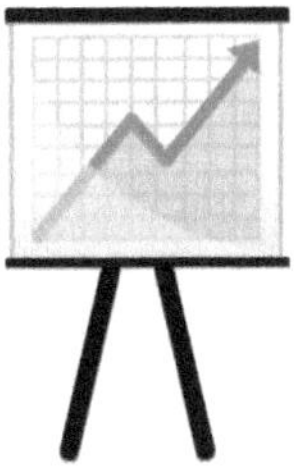

Portfolio at Age 51

- Roth IRA = $408,923
- Piggy Bank = $35,400
- House = $208,500
- Car = $9,000

Total Portfolio Value = $661,823

Chapter 33

Age 52

Income per year = $45,000

Income per month = $3,750

- Give 10% of income to charity = $375 per month
- Contribute $250 per month to Roth IRA
- Put $50 per month in Piggy Bank

Money left over per month for expenses and taxes = $3,075

Portfolio at Age 52

- Roth IRA = $448,726
- Piggy Bank = $36,000
- House = $209,000
- Car = $8,000

Total Portfolio Value = $701,726

Chapter 34

Age 53

Income per year = $45,000

Income per month = $3,750

- Give 10% of income to charity = $375 per month
- Contribute $250 per month to Roth IRA
- Put $50 per month in Piggy Bank

Money left over per month for expenses and taxes = $3,075

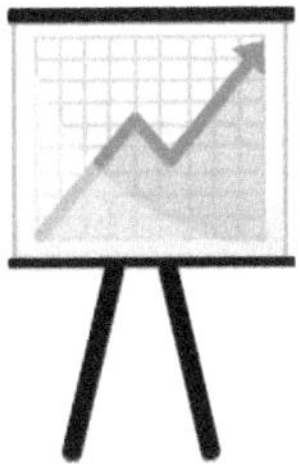

Portfolio at Age 53

- Roth IRA = $492,111
- Piggy Bank = $36,600
- House = $209,500
- Car = $7,000

Total Portfolio Value = $745,211

Chapter 35

Age 54

Income per year = $45,000

Income per month = $3,750

- Give 10% of income to charity = $375 per month
- Contribute $250 per month to Roth IRA
- Put $50 per month in Piggy Bank

Money left over per month for expenses and taxes = $3,075

Portfolio at Age 54

- Roth IRA = $539,401
- Piggy Bank = $37,200
- House = $210,000
- Car = $6,000

Total Portfolio Value = $792,601

Chapter 36

Age 55

Income per year = $45,000

Income per month = $3,750

- Give 10% of income to charity = $375 per month
- Contribute $250 per month to Roth IRA
- Put $50 per month in Piggy Bank

Money left over per month for expenses and taxes = $3,075

Portfolio at Age 55

Roth IRA = $590,947
Piggy Bank = $37,800
House = $210,500
Car = $5,000

Total Portfolio Value = $844,247

Chapter 37

Age 56

Income per year = $45,000

Income per month = $3,750

- Give 10% of income to charity = $375 per month
- Contribute $250 per month to Roth IRA
- Put $50 per month in Piggy Bank

Money left over per month for expenses and taxes = $3,075

Portfolio at Age 56

- Roth IRA = $647,132
- Piggy Bank = $38,400
- House = $211,000
- Car = $4,000

Total Portfolio Value = $900,532

Chapter 38

Age 57

Income per year = $45,000

Income per month = $3,750

- Give 10% of income to charity = $375 per month
- Contribute $250 per month to Roth IRA
- Put $50 per month in Piggy Bank

Money left over per month for expenses and taxes = $3,075

Portfolio at Age 57

- Roth IRA = $708,374
- Piggy Bank = $39,000
- House = $211,500
- Car = $3,000

Total Portfolio Value = $961,874

Chapter 39

Age 58

Income per year = $45,000

Income per month = $3,750

- Give 10% of income to charity = $375 per month
- Contribute $250 per month to Roth IRA

Money left over per month for expenses and taxes = $3,125

Portfolio at Age 58

- Roth IRA = $775,128
- Piggy Bank = $39,000
- House = $212,000
- Car = $2,000

Total Portfolio Value = $1,028,128

Chapter 40

Age 59

Income per year = $45,000

Income per month = $3,750

- Give 10% of income to charity = $375 per month
- Contribute $250 per month to Roth IRA

Money left over per month for expenses and taxes = $3,125

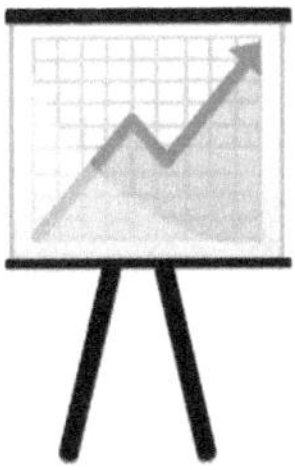

Portfolio at Age 59

- Roth IRA = $847,889
- Piggy Bank = $39,000
- House = $212,500
- Car = $1,000

Total Portfolio Value = $1,100,389

Chapter 41

Age 60

Income per year = $45,000

Income per month = $3,750

- Give 10% of income to charity = $375 per month
- Contribute $250 per month to Roth IRA

Money left over per month for expenses and taxes = $3,125

Portfolio at Age 60

- Roth IRA = $927,889
- Piggy Bank = $39,000
- House = $213,000

Total Portfolio Value = $1,179,199

Chapter 42

Age 61

Income per year = $45,000

Income per month = $3,750

- Give 10% of income to charity = $375 per month
- Contribute $250 per month to Roth IRA

Money left over per month for expenses and taxes = $3,125

Portfolio at Age 61

- Roth IRA = $1,013,647
- Piggy Bank = $39,000
- House = $213,500

Total Portfolio Value = $1,266,147

Chapter 43

Age 62

Income withdrawn tax-free from Roth IRA per year = $48,000

Tax-free income per month = $4,000

- Retire from Truck Driving career
- Give 10% of income to charity = $400 per month
- Buy a $400,000 condo on the beach with cash withdrawn tax-free from Roth IRA
- Buy a $100,000 RV Camper with cash withdrawn tax-free from Roth IRA

Money left over per month for expenses = $3,600

Portfolio at Age 62

- Roth IRA = $556,876
- Piggy Bank = $39,000
- House = $214,000
- Condo on the beach = $400,000
- RV Camper = $100,000

Total Portfolio Value = $1,309,876

Chapter 44

Age 63

Income withdrawn tax-free from Roth IRA per year = $48,000

Tax-free income per month = $4,000

- Give 10% of income to charity = $400 per month

Money left over per month for expenses = $3,600

Portfolio at Age 63

- Roth IRA = $558,944
- Piggy Bank = $39,000
- House = $214,500
- Condo on the beach = $400,500
- RV Camper = $99,000

Total Portfolio Value = $1,311,994

Chapter 45

Age 64

Income withdrawn tax-free from Roth IRA per year = $48,000

- Give 10% of income to charity = $400 per month

Money left over per month for expenses = $3,600

Portfolio at Age 64

- Roth IRA = $561,304
- Piggy Bank = $39,000
- House = $215,000
- Condo on the beach = $401,000
- RV Camper = $98,000

Total Portfolio Value = $1,314,304

Chapter 46

Age 65

Income withdrawn tax-free from Roth IRA per year = $48,000

Tax-free income per month = $4,000

- Give 10% of income to charity = $400 per month

Money left over per month for expenses = $3,600

Portfolio at Age 65

- Roth IRA = $563,821
- Piggy Bank = $39,000
- House = $215,500
- Condo on the beach = $401,500
- RV Camper = $97,000

Total Portfolio Value = $1,316,821

Chapter 47

Age 66

Income withdrawn tax-free from Roth IRA per year = $48,000

Tax-free income per month = $4,000

- Give 10% of income to charity = $400 per month

Money left over per month for expenses = $3,600

Portfolio at Age 66

- Roth IRA = $566,821
- Piggy Bank = $39,000
- House = $216,000
- Condo on the beach = $402,000
- RV Camper = $96,000

Total Portfolio Value = $1,319,565

Chapter 48

Age 67

Income withdrawn tax-free from Roth IRA per year = $48,000

Tax-free income per month = $4,000

- Give 10% of income to charity = $400 per month

Money left over per month for expenses = $3,600

Portfolio at Age 67

- Roth IRA = $569,556
- Piggy Bank = $39,000
- House = $216,500
- Condo on the beach = $402,500
- RV Camper = $95,000

Total Portfolio Value = $1,322,556

Chapter 49

Age 68

Income withdrawn tax-free from Roth IRA per year = $48,000

Tax-free income per month = $4,000

- Give 10% of income to charity = $400 per month

Money left over per month for expenses = $3,600

Portfolio at Age 68

- Roth IRA = $572,816
- Piggy Bank = $39,000
- House = $217,000
- Condo on the beach = $403,000
- RV Camper = $94,000

Total Portfolio Value = $1,325,816

Chapter 50

Age 69

Income withdrawn tax-free from Roth IRA per year = $48,000

Tax-free income per month = $4,000

- Give 10% of income to charity = $400 per month

Money left over per month for expenses = $3,600

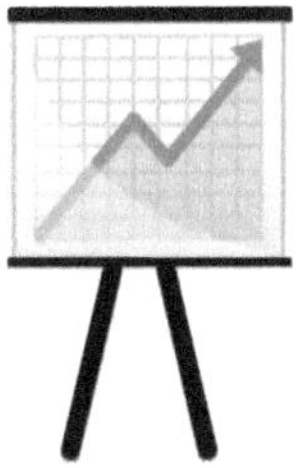

Portfolio at Age 69

- Roth IRA = $576,370
- Piggy Bank = $39,000
- House = $217,500
- Condo on the beach = $403,500
- RV Camper = $93,000

Total Portfolio Value = $1,329,370

Chapter 51

Age 70

Income withdrawn tax-free from Roth IRA per year = $48,000

Tax-free income per month = $4,000

- Give 10% of income to charity = $400 per month

Money left over per month for expenses = $3,600

Portfolio at Age 70

- Roth IRA = $580,243
- Piggy Bank = $39,000
- House = $218,000
- Condo on the beach = $404,000
- RV Camper = $92,000

Total Portfolio Value = $1,333,243

Chapter 52

Age 71

Income withdrawn tax-free from Roth IRA per year = $48,000

Tax-free income per month = $4,000

- Give 10% of income to charity = $400 per month

Money left over per month for expenses = $3,600

Portfolio at Age 71

- Roth IRA = $584,465
- Piggy Bank = $39,000
- House = $218,500
- Condo on the beach = $404,500
- RV Camper = $91,000

Total Portfolio Value = $1,337,465

Chapter 53

Age 72

Income withdrawn tax-free from Roth IRA per year = $48,000

Tax-free income per month = $4,000

- Give 10% of income to charity = $400 per month

Money left over per month for expenses = $3,600

Portfolio at Age 72

Roth IRA = $589,066
Piggy Bank = $39,000
House = $219,000
Condo on the beach = $405,000
RV Camper = $90,000

Total Portfolio Value = $1,342,066

Chapter 54

Age 73

Income withdrawn tax-free from Roth IRA per year = $48,000

Tax-free income per month = $4,000

- Give 10% of income to charity = $400 per month

Money left over per month for expenses = $3,600

Portfolio at Age 73

- Roth IRA = $594,082
- Piggy Bank = $39,000
- House = $219,500
- Condo on the beach = $405,500
- RV Camper = $89,000

Total Portfolio Value = $1,347,082

Chapter 55

Age 74

Income withdrawn tax-free from Roth IRA per year = $48,000

Tax-free income per month = $4,000

- Give 10% of income to charity = $400 per month

Money left over per month for expenses = $3,600

Portfolio at Age 74

- Roth IRA = $599,550
- Piggy Bank = $39,000
- House = $220,000
- Condo on the beach = $406,000
- RV Camper = $88,000

Total Portfolio Value = $1,352,550

Chapter 56

Age 75

Income withdrawn tax-free from Roth IRA per year = $48,000

Tax-free income per month = $4,000

- Give 10% of income to charity = $400 per month

Money left over per month for expenses = $3,600

Portfolio at Age 75

- Roth IRA = $605,509
- Piggy Bank = $39,000
- House = $220,500
- Condo on the beach = $406,500
- RV Camper = $87,000

Total Portfolio Value = $1,358,509

Chapter 57

Conclusion

I hope this eBook has given you a snapshot of what could be. I'll repeat "The 5 Rules to Follow". Try to enjoy the journey, not just the destination.

The 5 Rules to Follow

1. Give 10% of your income to your favorite charity. Why? Because it gives you the sense of abundance. It's a nice thing to do. It's giving back. In general, the more you give, the more you receive. It's giving thanks to the Higher Power. If you're a believer, it's giving thanks to God.

2. Contribute $250 every month to a Roth IRA (Individual Retirement Account). Invest this money in the Vanguard Total Stock Market Index Mutual Fund at https://investor.vanguard.com/home/. This investment has very low costs and has returned over 9% interest per year since its inception in 1992. In Joe's case, his investments returned an average of 9% interest per year. If the stock market is down, keep investing monthly. If the stock market is up, keep investing monthly.
3. Never borrow money. Pay cash for everything. Rent until you can buy it with cash.
4. Live below your means. Spend less than you make. Don't waste your hard earned money. Be frugal. Be creative. Sacrifice some luxuries now and hopefully you can enjoy them in abundance later without digging yourself into a hole.
5. Save money in your Piggy Bank for an emergency fund or an investment, such as a house.

Available at Amazon.com
(Paperback and Kindle versions)

More Stuff

Twitter: @byHawkeyeJohn (follow me & I'll follow you)

Facebook: facebook.com/hawkeye.john.writer (friend me)

Website & blog: hawkeyejohn.com (bookmark for What's New)

Pinterest: pinterest.com/HawkeyeJohn (I'll follow your boards)

www.ingramcontent.com/pod-product-compliance
Lightning Source LLC
Chambersburg PA
CBHW021433170526
45164CB00001B/232
9781494840181